Stop & Think!

Volume 2

150 Questions
That Will Transform Your
Relationships, Your
Community and Your Life

Steve Lieman

&

Doug Marden

Published by Stop & Think

8 Elm Street, Groton, MA 01450.

Copyright © 2017

by Steve Lieman and Doug Marden

First Edition – September 2017

All rights reserved

ISBN 978-1-387-20878-4

From the Talmud:

"Do not be daunted by the enormity of the world's grief.

Act justly, now.
Love mercy, now.
Walk humbly, now.

You are not obligated to complete the work, but neither are you free to abandon it."

Why Questions?

Even a single question applied to **the situation that concerns you most** has the power to transform that situation.

The problem we face is that in the heat of the moment we simply don't think of the questions that could help us the most.

Inside this book's covers you will find an assortment of potent questions: questions that are already powerful on their own but when taken together open up possibilities, empowering you to take action and get the results you want.

Quick Start: How to use this book

Stop & Think! Volume 2 has no beginning or end. Every page marks a fresh start, a place for you to record your insights.

This book is intended to be written in, not just read. It's your tool, a ready, convenient source of inspiration and ideas you can apply whenever you feel stuck or whenever you seek greater clarity.

For your specific situation, *Stop & Think! Volume 2* offers gentle help and insights every time you open it on whatever page you examine.

So, stop and think of the issue that is most occupying your thoughts, **the situation that concerns you most**.

Roll it over in your mind and write it down on the "Situation Page" that immediately precedes the main question section of this book.

Once you have clarified your basic situation, then that's the time to open the book to any question page and read each question as you turn to it until you see one that fits your needs.

Take your time.

Begin to answer that question in your mind thoughtfully and deeply. We encourage you to speak the answer aloud or repeat it silently to yourself.

Pause. Breathe. Let the answer take shape. And when you are ready, write it down. Shorthand, abbreviations or outline form are perfect for this task.

As you feel momentum from taking this first step, continue with the process and seek out additional questions that build on the first.

Come back often to dig deeper or to go broader -- opening up new possibilities for action and for creating the results you want in your life for yourself and for those around you whose lives your efforts will enrich.

Repeat this *Stop & Think!* process with any new situation or problem that arises for you, your relationships, or your community.

Even a single question thoughtfully answered has the power to redirect the course of history and to change lives for the better.

We wish you many blessings on your journey of discovery.

The Importance of Feedback Loops in Making the Best Use of Questions

The whole idea of this book revolves around literally **stopping** at regular intervals and then **thinking** by asking and answering a full mix of powerful questions.

We need to stop because success at moving things forward, capturing opportunities, and avoiding pitfalls demands we take stock regularly and repeatedly of the current situation. This lets us discover what has happened recently including whether any interventions we had previously initiated worked as planned.

No Silver Bullet. This book is not a silver bullet. No single question in this volume will make everything right for you. Even if you ask and answer all the best questions, the situation may not always work out perfectly to your advantage.

You are in Charge. To make best use of these questions, you and your teammates are going to have to make a series of mid-course corrections. You will need to turn on your best observational skills and figure out the key factors to monitor systematically and repeatedly. You will regularly have to reorient yourselves as new information becomes available. And then you will need to decide the best next steps after generating and evaluating a set of available options.

Stop & Think: Full Stop or Rolling Stop?
Stopping comes in two basic varieties, Full Stop and Rolling Stop (which is similar to what happens when you merge into traffic at a yield sign). Sometimes we have the luxury of taking a full stop. In that time period we have the opportunity to explore multiple interrelated questions.

The Full Stop Approach: Skim and Select.

When a full stop is possible, you might consider skimming through this volume and picking out, one by one, questions that appear in that moment to be helpful for your purpose. Then when you have assembled a handful (5 or 10 or 20), you can work your way through all of these questions and see how the answers interact and magnify the value and usefulness of any single question.

For best results, we suggest spending a minimum of 10 to 15 minutes and preferably 30 to 60 minutes at this task.

The authors used exactly this technique when we were stuck on some issues midway through this project. We were able to identify 17 questions that seemed to fit and then we spent about 45 minutes working our way through them, jotting down answers in abbreviated form.   By the time we finished, we were completely unstuck. We had a prioritized list of next steps that would once again give our project the momentum it needed.

We asked some of the early reviewers of this book to try this technique and they have told us how delighted they were in the way this approach helped them take on their most challenging situation. One of our reviewers told us that:

> *"The questions calmed down the situation for me and allowed me to pass on that calmness to some other participants. This led towards healing, something which was indispensable in my situation. For this situation, the question about how to keep lines of communication open proved especially helpful."*

For Rolling Stop: Be Prepared.

There are other circumstances when we don't or won't have the luxury of stopping fully. This is what we are calling a Rolling Stop. The Stop and Think questions in this book can still help, but you may only be able to deal with one or two at a time. So we recommend you plan ahead and select in advance a handful of your favorite "in the moment" questions from this book. Then practice having them at the ready so you can recall them for fast moving situations.

Some of our favorite questions of this type are:

- **What's next?** [helps maintain momentum]
- **Who benefits?** [helps identify hidden agendas]
- **What's missing?** [helps fill in the pieces of the puzzle]
- **What can't wait?** [helps encourage a sense of urgency]
- **What can we let go of right now?** [helps avoid overload]
- **What other choices do we have?** [helps increase our options]
- **What must we do to keep the lines of communication open?** [helps tap into the "wisdom in the room"]

As soon as a quiet moment arrives, that's the time to consciously take a Full Stop, select a set of questions that fit what just happened, and devote time to coming up with answers for a fuller understanding before making any further decisions.

It is important to realize that the Stop & Think! Questions are not intended to be "One and Done" saviors of the situation. We recommend getting into the habit of referring back to these questions regularly. As the situation changes over time, you will discover that a different mix of questions comes into play: questions that are more in synch with evolving conditions.

What Can Powerful Questions Do For You?

At Stop & Think! our core belief is that questions are our friends. Questions help us in countless ways including to:

- Let go of things we no longer need
- See more clearly into the nature of things
- Dig deeper into complex situations
- Help jump us out of a rut we are in
- Create more choices, options, alternatives
- Focus on the Main Event
- Remind us we need patience and persistence
- Set up positive self-fulfilling situations
- Pay attention to positive and negative energy
- Identify leverage points
- Tune in to the right timing & maintain momentum
- Build community
- Take care of ourselves
- Deliver necessary bad news in a timely fashion
- Adjust focus
- Gather facts
- Break away from complacency
- Provide a different perspective
- Challenge assumptions

Of course, that's a lot to pay attention to. We cannot do it all at once. And that brings us back to the purpose of this book: to gently remind us over time to ask and answer a full slate of questions.

What about really hard questions?

As you work with this book you will find that some of the questions that fit your situation are especially difficult to answer.

This may seem discouraging but don't despair. It turns out that hard-to-answer questions are excellent clues. These questions help us decide what aspects will benefit most from the investment of additional energy.

Similarly, questions you cannot answer at all offer further clues where to profitably focus and devote our attention.

We hope you are now ready to define and sketch out the situation that concerns you most, and then jump into the questions themselves and learn first-hand how they can help you take charge and move things forward.

Once you try this for one or two situations, we are confident you will return again and again to *Stop & Think! Volume 2*.

How to Make Best Use of the Stop & Think! Web Site

As an adjunct to your using the questions in this volume to help you focus on the situation that concerns you most, please look at the Stop & Think! web site (www.stopandthink.net).

The web site can offer up a new life-changing question every time you return to the site's home page. That way you can access powerful questions from your mobile device or desktop any time you are feeling stuck!

Stop & Think Situation Page
Taking Stock of the Situations
That Concern You Most

Briefly describe your situation.

What about this situation concerns you the most?

When did this situation arise?

Is it getting better or worse or is it stuck in place?

Who are the key players, the key stakeholders? How will we keep track of their preferences, beliefs, values, needs, biases, rules, agendas, etc.?

What agreements or covenants have we made for our team? How can we strengthen these?

How important is it to get this right? What's at stake? How can you quantify this?

Continued on next page

Taking Stock ...

How committed are you? How motivated are you to invest your time and energy?

What's your role?

Who is depending on you?

Whose lives will be impacted by what does or does not happen?

How soon must this be resolved?

What has this already cost us?

What resources do you have at your disposal?

How are you tracking progress?

Stop & Think!

Volume 2

150 Questions
That Will Transform Your
Relationships, Your Community
and Your Life

Which questions fit your situation
the best?

What's great about this mess?

What's worked before
in this kind of situation?

What is my gut telling me?

What isn't quite the way we want it yet?

What would "winning" look like?

What needs our urgent attention?

What can we let go of right now?

Who can we count on to be there for us?

Who is not playing fair?

What are the alternatives?

What important signs are we failing to notice? *

How can we simplify this?

How is this
an opportunity in disguise?

What's missing?

What can I change that will prove helpful to this other person?

Who else can help?

What just doesn't add up?

Who benefits from this?

How will we make the time?

How can I explain this in 25 words or less?

Who has my back? Who is always watching out for my interests?

Who else can help us now?

What's next?

What no longer serves us?

Where can doing less help more?

What have I
been missing all along?

What must we say "NO" to now?

What must we schedule time for today?

Where's the common ground? *

* *When emotional energy and the chance for conflict are high, this has proven to be a powerful door-opening question.*

What mid-course correction is needed right now?

What can we leave out?

What conclusions
can we draw so far?

What can I improve on right now?

How will we track progress?

Who knows best?

Who's been blowing smoke and trying to fool us?

What warning lights are flashing?

Who from our past
could help us now?

Why wait?
What can we do right now?

Who should we listen to now?

How can we build on this?

What will shake us out of this rut?

What are the elephants in the room? What obvious problem or risk have we been avoiding discussing?

What will open up even more choices for us?

What needs of mine
are not being met right now?
How does that make me feel?

How do we make sure bad news gets delivered promptly so we can act on it quickly?

What assumptions are we making? How do we plan to verify them?

Where can I find a quiet place to gather my thoughts?

What can we put on the back burner for now?

Who can provide a second opinion? Who else can we get to weigh in?

What's the best way to keep this ball rolling?

What must we stop doing right now?

What do we see
that others cannot?

How can I help the group most in the next few days? What can I do or change now that doesn't depend on anyone else?

At this crossroad,
what options are available?

What patterns have recently emerged?

If our current approach doesn't pan out, what's our plan B?

How can I change in ways that would make a difference?

What's the most essential thing? How will keeping this in mind help me to stay focused?

What have we learned from this setback?

How can we make this easier and more palatable for that other person?

What must be allowed
to unfold at its own pace?

Who else can we invite to participate?

What's our top priority?

Who makes me smile?

Where can we give more than expected?

What small change will make a difference now?

Who deserves our thanks?

Any recent surprises?
How can we use them?

What is my intuition telling me?

What distractions are slowing us down and must be pushed aside?

What can we do now
that we could not do before?

What's changed
since our last evaluation?
How does it affect our plan?

What will help
build team morale?

What else must we pay attention to now?

What's my mood right now? Mad? Glad? Sad? Scared? How does this affect my approach to the situation?

What excess baggage
is slowing us down?

What else can we learn from this situation?

What options haven't been accounted for yet?

How can urgency
work to our advantage?

What can we do together that we can't do alone?

Who can help us avoid being overly optimistic? Who is best suited to look at the situation from all sides and evaluate all the different possibilities?

What would make our case more compelling?

How will we make our results more visible?

What needs rehearsal before sharing more widely?

What will have
the greatest impact?

What other choices do we have?

Who must we add to the list of stakeholders?

What other patterns can we find in the data?

What detail have we missed?

What changes are needed?

What would our hero do now?

How do we free up time to focus on the really important stuff?

What will go best
if left to others?

How will we keep score?

How can we
look at this differently?

What sacrifices are we willing to make now to move this forward?

What have we selected as our key indicators of progress?

What manipulation is under way and by whom?
How do I feel about it? *

* If manipulations are going on, this is a question you are going to want to return to again and again to make sure you are seeing things straight.

What else would we risk if we knew we could not fail?

How can we handle this situation without causing more trouble?

What other possible options are there?

How did things change today?

How can we turn the tables now?

What parts are non-negotiable?

What new alternatives
can we invent?

What great things happened today?

What still doesn't make sense?

What's been distracting us from the main event?

What's the bright side of this?

Who has proven unreliable? *

* For example, who has shown bad judgment? proven
themselves a manipulator? blamed others? or
systematically created emotional conflicts?

What have we learned so far that clarifies our goals?

What don't we have to wait for any more?

What other resources can we bring to bear?

Who can we
absolutely depend on?

If it feels like I am wearing too many hats, which can I safely drop?

What can help us see ourselves more clearly?

Which of our assumptions might be wrong?

Who are our most reliable informants?

What's the unstated agenda?

How will we
add to our momentum?

What's not working quite to plan?

What's the main event?

What do we wish we had done differently? What did we learn? How will we use that?

What must we not put off till tomorrow?

What's holding us back?

What things are best left alone?

Why does this matter?

What else can we notice?

What's our safety net if things don't work out?

How can we illustrate our point even better?

What matters most?

What conclusions can we draw?

What benefits could I realize if I stopped trying so hard?

What have we learned today?

Who would be best
to consult about this?

What follow up action must we take today?

What part can we delegate?

What am I waiting for?

Who can light the way?

What's in it for them?

What are we taking for granted?

If now, how? If not now, when?

What must we do to keep the lines of communication open? *

* If you are working in a team, this is a question that you will want to return to on a regular basis.

What can't wait?

What are we overlooking?

How must I change now in order to become even more effective?

To what are we absolutely committed?

What questions can I invent for myself?

What other important situations are ripe for the Stop & Think! approach?

Stop & Think Situation Page
Taking Stock of the Situations
That Concern You Most

Briefly describe your situation.

What about this situation concerns you the most?

When did this situation arise?

Is it getting better or worse or is it stuck in place?

Who are the key players, the key stakeholders? How will we keep track of their preferences, beliefs, values, needs, biases, rules, agendas, etc.?

What agreements or covenants have we made for our team? How can we strengthen these?

How important is it to get this right? What's at stake? How can you quantify this?

Continued on next page

Taking Stock ...

How committed are you? How motivated are you to invest your time and energy?

What's your role?

Who is depending on you?

Whose lives will be impacted by what does or does not happen?

How soon must this be resolved?

What has this already cost us?

What resources do you have at your disposal?

How are you tracking progress?

Stop & Think Situation Page
Taking Stock of the Situations
That Concern You Most

Briefly describe your situation.

What about this situation concerns you the most?

When did this situation arise?

Is it getting better or worse or is it stuck in place?

Who are the key players, the key stakeholders? How will we keep track of their preferences, beliefs, values, needs, biases, rules, agendas, etc.?

What agreements or covenants have we made for our team? How can we strengthen these?

How important is it to get this right? What's at stake? How can you quantify this?

Continued on next page

Taking Stock ...

How committed are you? How motivated are you to invest your time and energy?

What's your role?

Who is depending on you?

Whose lives will be impacted by what does or does not happen?

How soon must this be resolved?

What has this already cost us?

What resources do you have at your disposal?

How are you tracking progress?

Stop & Think Situation Page
Taking Stock of the Situations
That Concern You Most

Briefly describe your situation.

What about this situation concerns you the most?

When did this situation arise?

Is it getting better or worse or is it stuck in place?

Who are the key players, the key stakeholders? How will we keep track of their preferences, beliefs, values, needs, biases, rules, agendas, etc.?

What agreements or covenants have we made for our team? How can we strengthen these?

How important is it to get this right? What's at stake? How can you quantify this?

Continued on next page

Taking Stock ...

How committed are you? How motivated are you to invest your time and energy?

What's your role?

Who is depending on you?

Whose lives will be impacted by what does or does not happen?

How soon must this be resolved?

What has this already cost us?

What resources do you have at your disposal?

How are you tracking progress?

The Story Behind the Book

How and why did Doug and Steve begin their search for the best, most powerful, most useful questions?

It began in 1989 when Steve developed a technique he called the *Performance Audit Litany (PAL).* This was a series of relatively simple questions that could be used as a quick start systems trouble shooting tool for computer system performance. Using PAL, a performance analyst could gain a breadth of understanding in just a few minutes. This provided a solid foundation to jump-start the investigation and profitably focus attention.

The following year Steve and Doug discovered Tony Robbins, author of *Awaken the Giant Within,* and many other bestselling books. Through Tony they discovered the power of good questions. They developed ideas on what made a good question and which questions were self-defeating. They learned to avoid questions that could be answered with a simple yes or no. They discovered that the way you frame a question has the power to take you in either a positive or negative direction and how to make sure you stick with the positive frame. They sought out and examined problem solving questions and daily inspiration questions and even quotations that they could turn into powerful questions.

As they learned the power of developing and asking the right questions, they were also aware of the dangers of forgetting to ask questions.

In 1991, Doug and Steve started talking about how they might create something that would make it easier for ordinary mortals to remember to ask a full mix of questions to move things forward. They toyed with the idea of a card deck or a book with the best questions, something you could carry with you and consult sequentially or at random as necessary.

For the next ten years, they collected thousands of questions, and evaluated them for how powerful they might be. They continued selecting and refining the questions until they had gathered a collection of the ones they thought were best.

In 1999, Steve and Doug created the *Stop & Think* web site www.stopandthink.net that included many of their best questions. These questions could be accessed randomly each time you returned to the Home Page or refreshed your browser window.

For the next decade, they continued to select, refine, and prune the best questions, evaluating literally thousands of questions in the process.

Finally in 2011 after twenty years of effort they published *Stop & Think: Questions That Will Change Your Life*, containing 101 of their most powerful questions, with **a focus on changing the lives of individual readers**.

In 2017, Steve and Doug started work on this book, *Stop & Think!, Volume 2*, with a focus on creating questions for use by individuals, by families and by groups that would help them in the situations that concerned them the most and that would support them in **changing themselves, their relationships, their organizations, and their communities**.

Please write to us!

If you have a question of your own that has brought change in your life or helped you deal effectively with a challenging situation, please send it on to us at Stop & Think, 8 Elm Street, Groton, MA 01450. We are interested in the ways these questions have helped you and the results you have achieved.

If you are feeling stuck, please check out our website www.stopandthink.net. This is a handy source of useful questions. You can access them instantly any time you are online at your desk or on your mobile device. Each time you return to the home page you will get a new Stop & Think question – maybe just the one you were looking for.

Keep going until you find one that feels right for the situation you are most concerned with and see how it can help you get unstuck.

About the Authors

Steve Lieman and Doug Marden live in Massachusetts. They are authors and speakers who have used questions extensively and to their advantage in their Computer Systems work in the USA and abroad, and in their personal lives.

They have been actively studying questions together for the past 26 years, searching for questions that provide the greatest power and leverage. This book and the previously published **Stop & Think! Volume 1** are the fruits of this labor.

NOTES

NOTES